Book of the Watchers

By Enoch

ISBN: 978-1-63118-615-8

Other Books in this Series and Related Titles

The Book of Wisdom of Solomon by King Solomon (978-1-63118-502-1)

The Apocalypse of Peter by Peter (978-1-63118-527-4)

The Gospel of the Nativity of Mary by St. Matthew (978-1-63118-448-2)

The Vision of Saint Paul the Apostle by Paul (978-1-63118-526-7)

Early Translation of the Acts of the Apostles by Luke (978-1-63118-521-2)

The Hymn of Jesus by G. R. S. Mead (978-1-63118-409-3)

Psalms of Solomon by King Solomon (978-1-63118-439-0)

The First and Second Gospels of the Infancy of Jesus Christ (978-1-63118-415-4)

The Book of Parables by Enoch (978-1-63118-429-1)

The Testament of Abraham by Abraham (978-1-63118-441-3)

The Lives of Adam and Eve by Moses (978-1-63118-414-7)

Fourth Book of Maccabees by Josephus (978-1-63118-562-5)

The Secrets of Enoch by Enoch (978-1-63118-449-9)

Lost Chapters of the Book of Daniel and Related Writings (978-1-63118-417-8)

The Testament of Moses by Moses (978-1-63118-440-6)

Testaments of the Twelve Patriarchs (978-1-63118-579-3)

The Story of Ahikar by Ahiqar (978-1-63118-561-8)

The Odes of Solomon by King Solomon (978-1-63118-503-8)

Book of Dreams by Enoch (978-1-63118-437-6)

Kali the Mother by Sister Nivedita (978-1-63118-558-8)

The Book of Astronomical Secrets by Enoch (978-1-63118-443-7)

Audio Versions are also Available on Audible, Amazon and Apple

Other Books in this Series and Related Titles

The Hidden Mysteries of Christianity by Annie Besant (978–1–63118–534–2)

Rosicrucian Rules, Secret Signs, Codes and Symbols by various (978-1-63118-488-8)

The Hymns of Hermes by G. R. S. Mead (978-1-63118-405-5)

Freemasonry and the Egyptian Mysteries by C. W. Leadbeater (978-1-63118-456-7)

The Sepher Yetzirah and the Qabalah by M P Hall (978-1-63118-481-9)

Love and Death by Sri Aurobindo (978-1-63118-557-1)

The Historic, Mythic and Mystic Christ by Annie Besant (978–1–63118–533–5)

The Fourth-Gospel and Synoptical Problem by G R S Mead (978–1–63118–576–2)

Masonic Symbolism of King Solomon's Temple by A Mackey &c (978-1-63118-442-0)

The Crest-Jewel of Wisdom by Adi Shankara (978-1-63118-475-8)

The Old Past Master by Carl H Claudy (978-1-63118-464-2)

The Brotherhood of Religions by Annie Besant (978–1–63118–563–2)

What Theosophy Does for Us by C W Leadbeater (978–1–63118–574–8)

Buddhist Psalms by Shinran (978-1-63118-465-9)

Catholicism, Yoga and Hinduism by Hartmann &c (978-1-63118-478-9)

Masonic Symbolism of Easter and the Christ in Masonry (978-1-63118-434-5)

Tao Te Ching & Commentary by Lao Tzu & C Johnston (978-1-63118-495-6)

Ancient Mysteries and Secret Societies by M P Hall (978-1-63118-410-9)

The Golden Verses of Pythagoras: Five Translations (978-1-63118-479-6)

Freemasonry & Catholicism by Max Heindel (978-1-63118-508-3)

A Few Masonic Sermons by A. C. Ward &c (978-1-63118-435-2)

Audio versions are also available on Audible, Amazon and Apple

Table of Contents

PROLOGUE

Who is Enoch and why is he so important?

Jude 1:14 describes Enoch as being the seventh generation of man from Adam, while also making reference to Enoch's ability to prophesize. Enoch was born on Seth's side of Adam and Eve's lineage and was the great grandfather of Noah. References to him in the Bible are sparse, but he is most well known for not having died but instead for having walked away with God. In some Christian and Jewish traditions Enoch is also considered to be a scribe and to have been ordained as a priest by Adam.

Perhaps because of Enoch's unique departure from Earth into heaven, there was a rich tradition of exploring what Enoch's life was like, upon leaving Earth. The events of his time in heaven were often explored in classic rabbinical literature as well as the three primary apocryphal books with his name attached to them. Some modern churches continue to embrace Enoch's importance, including the Ethiopian Orthodox Church and perhaps more notably, the Latter Day Saints.

The full text of the magnum opus commonly known as *The Book of Enoch* or *1 Enoch*, is in fact a collection of five separate and unrelated, apocryphal books, the authorship of which spanned several centuries in history, while the real commonality of all being that they each involve Enoch.

That, which is usually presented as the first 36 chapters of *The Book of Enoch* was originally known as the **Book of the Watchers** and is actually only the second oldest of the five collected texts, dating to around 200 B.C. This translation of the *Book of the Watchers* comes to us from notable scholar of apocryphal literature, R. H. Charles, who published it in 1917.

The narrative of the *Book of the Watchers* is told from the point of view of Enoch and not surprisingly focuses on a class of angels known as the Watchers. Watchers are featured in the fourth chapter of the Book of Daniel as well as some of the other apocryphal books that have Enoch's name attached to them.

The Watchers were angels who decided to transgress the boundaries of mankind, as set by God and instead became enamored with the daughters of men and took those women as their wives. Their hybrid children, half angel and half human were called the Nephilim; they were often described as giants, and are referenced in the sixth chapter of the Book of Genesis.

Here, the Watchers, fearful of the consequences of their actions, call upon Enoch and ask him to intervene on their behalf, after their children, the Nephilim, begin killing men. Instead, with the aide of four of the seven archangels, Michael, Uriel, Raphael, and Gabriel, Enoch is charged by God with the task of issuing judgments of doom on the Watchers for their transgressions.

The book concludes with a series of journeys taken by Enoch, in which he describes the places of punishment for these angel sinners, their children and any who are not righteous.

R. H. Charles has this to say about the imagery seen in Enoch's journeys,

> *"The fallen angels were believed to have brought sin on to the earth; all the wickedness of the world the Apocalyptist traces back to them. This cause of sin must be wholly destroyed before righteousness can come truly to its own. Therefore the Apocalyptist has a practical aim in view when describing in much detail the final place of punishment of the fallen angels; for here, too, are to come all those who by sin are the offspring of this race. No less does he delight in telling of the abode of joy prepared for the righteous. That all these descriptions were constructed out of the imagination of the Apocalyptist, based largely, no doubt, upon popular tradition, did not detract from their practical value for the people of his day. He was a preacher of righteousness who looked forward in absolute conviction to the final overthrow of sin; and all his visions have as their motive-power the yearning for and belief in the triumph of righteousness over sin."*

Book of the Watchers

Part I

The Parable of Enoch on the Future Lot of the Wicked and the Righteous

The words of the blessing of Enoch, wherewith he blessed the elect and righteous, who will be living in the day of tribulation, when all the wicked and godless are to be removed.

And he took up his parable and said--Enoch a righteous man, whose eyes were opened by God, saw the vision of the Holy One in the heavens, which the angels showed me, and from them I heard everything, and from them I understood as I saw, but not for this generation, but for a remote one which is for to come.

Concerning the elect I said, and took up my parable concerning them:

> The Holy Great One will come forth from His dwelling,
> And the eternal God will tread upon the earth, even on Mount Sinai,
> And appear from His camp
> And appear in the strength of His might from the heaven of heavens.

And all shall be smitten with fear
And the Watchers shall quake,
And great fear and trembling shall seize them unto the ends of the
earth.

And the high mountains shall be shaken,
And the high hills shall be made low,
And shall melt like wax before the flame

And the earth shall be wholly rent in sunder,
And all that is upon the earth shall perish,
And there shall be a judgment upon all men.

But with the righteous He will make peace.

And will protect the elect,
And mercy shall be upon them.

And they shall all belong to God,
And they shall be prospered,
And they shall all be blessed.

And He will help them all,
And light shall appear unto them,
And He will make peace with them.

And behold! He cometh with ten thousands of His holy ones
To execute judgment upon all,
And to destroy all the ungodly,

And to convict all flesh
Of all the works of their ungodliness which they have ungodly
committed,
And of all the hard things which ungodly sinners have spoken
against Him.

Observe ye everything that takes place in the heaven, how they do not change their orbits, and the luminaries which are in the heaven, how they all rise and set in order each in its season, and transgress not against their appointed order.

Behold ye the earth, and give heed to the things which take place upon it from first to last, how steadfast they are, how none of the things upon earth change, but all the works of God appear to you.

Behold the summer and the winter, how the whole earth is filled with water, and clouds and dew and rain lie upon it.

Observe and see how in the winter all the trees seem as though they had withered and shed all their leaves, except fourteen trees, which do not lose their foliage but retain the old foliage from two to three years till the new comes.

And again, observe ye the days of summer how the sun is above the earth over against it. And you seek shade and shelter by reason of the heat of the sun, and the earth also burns with growing heat, and so you cannot tread on the earth, or on a rock by reason of its heat.

Observe ye how the trees cover themselves with green leaves and bear fruit, wherefore give ye heed and know with regard to all His works, and recognize how He that liveth forever hath made them so.

And all His works go on thus from year to year forever, and all the tasks, which they accomplish for Him, and their tasks change not, but according as God hath ordained so is it done.

And behold how the sea and the rivers in like manner accomplish and change not their tasks from His commandments.

> But ye--ye have not been steadfast, nor done the commandments
> of the Lord,
> But ye have turned away and spoken proud and hard words
> With your impure mouths against His greatness.
> Oh, ye hard-hearted, ye shall find no peace.

> Therefore shall ye execrate your days,
> And the years of your life shall perish,
> And the years of your destruction shall be multiplied in eternal
> execration,
> And ye shall find no mercy.

> In those days ye shall make your names an eternal execration unto
> all the righteous,
> And all the sinners and godless shall imprecate by you,
> And for all of you sinners there shall be no salvation,
> But on you all shall abide a curse.

> But for the elect there shall be light and joy and peace,
> And all the righteous shall rejoice,
> There shall be salvation unto them, a goodly light.
> And there shall be forgiveness of sins,
> And every mercy and peace and forbearance
> And they shall inherit the earth.

> And then there shall be bestowed upon the elect wisdom,
> And they shall all live and never again sin,
> Either through ungodliness or through pride

But they who are wise shall be humble.

And they shall not again transgress,
Nor shall they sin all the days of their life,
Nor shall they die of the divine anger or wrath,
But they shall complete the number of the days of their life.

And their lives shall be increased in peace,
And the years of their joy shall be multiplied,
In eternal gladness and peace,
All the days of their life.

Part II

The Fall of the Angels

The Demoralization of Mankind

The Intercession of the Angels on Behalf of Mankind

The Dooms Pronounced by God on the Angels of the Messianic Kingdom

And it came to pass when the children of men had multiplied that in those days were born unto them beautiful and comely daughters.

And the angels, the children of the heaven, saw and lusted after them, and said to one another:

> *'Come, let us choose us wives from among the children of men and beget us children.'*

And Semjaza, who was their leader, said unto them:

> *'I fear ye will not indeed agree to do this deed, and I alone shall have to pay the penalty of a great sin.'*

And they all answered him and said:

'Let us all swear an oath, and all bind ourselves by mutual imprecations not to abandon this plan but to do this thing.'

Then swore they all together and bound themselves by mutual imprecations upon it.

And they were in all two hundred; who descended in the days of Jared on the summit of Mount Hermon, and they called it Mount Hermon, because they had sworn and bound themselves by mutual imprecations upon it.

And these are the names of the leaders: Semjaza, their leader, and Arakiba, Rameel, Kokabiel, Tamiel, Ramiel, Danel, Ezeqeel, Baraqijal, Asael, Armaros, Batarel, Ananel, Zaqiel, Samsapeel, Satarel, Turel, Jomjael, Sariel and more.

And these are their chiefs of tens.

And all the others together with them took unto themselves wives, and each chose for himself one, and they began to go in unto them and to defile themselves with them, and they taught them charms and enchantments, and the cutting of roots, and made them acquainted with plants.

And they became pregnant, and they bore great giants, whose height was three thousand ells, and who consumed all the acquisitions of men.

And when men could no longer sustain them, the giants

turned against them and devoured mankind.

And they began to sin against birds, and beasts, and reptiles, and fish, and to devour one another's flesh, and drink the blood.

Then the earth laid accusation against the lawless ones.

And Azazel taught men to make swords, and knives, and shields, and breastplates, and made known to them the metals of the earth and the art of working them, and bracelets, and ornaments, and the use of antimony, and the beautifying of the eyelids, and all kinds of costly stones, and all coloring tinctures.

And there arose much godlessness, and they committed fornication, and they were led astray, and became corrupt in all their ways. Semjaza taught enchantments, and root-cuttings, Armaros the resolving of enchantments, Baraqijal taught astrology, Kokabiel the constellations, Ezeqeel the knowledge of the clouds, Araqiel the signs of the earth, Shamsiel the signs of the sun, and Sariel the course of the moon. And as men perished, they cried, and their cry went up to heaven . . .

And then Michael, Uriel, Raphael, and Gabriel looked down from heaven and saw much blood being shed upon the earth, and all lawlessness being wrought upon the earth.

And they said one to another:

> *'The earth made without inhabitant cries the voice of their crying up to the gates of heaven. And now to you, the holy ones*

of heaven, the souls of men make their suit, saying, "Bring our cause before the Most High".'

And they said to the Lord of the ages:

'Lord of lords, God of gods, King of kings, and God of the ages, the throne of Thy glory standeth unto all the generations of the ages, and Thy name holy and glorious and blessed unto all the ages!

Thou hast made all things, and power over all things hast Thou, and all things are naked and open in Thy sight, and Thou seest all things, and nothing can hide itself from Thee.

Thou seest what Azazel hath done, who hath taught all unrighteousness on earth and revealed the eternal secrets which were preserved in heaven, which men were striving to learn.

And Semjaza, to whom Thou hast given authority to bear rule over his associates.

And they have gone to the daughters of men upon the earth, and have slept with the women, and have defiled themselves, and revealed to them all kinds of sins.

And the women have borne giants, and the whole earth has thereby been filled with blood and unrighteousness.

And now, behold, the souls of those who have died are crying and making their suit to the gates of heaven, and their lamentations have ascended, and cannot cease because of the lawless deeds which are wrought on the earth.

And Thou knowest all things before they come to pass, and Thou seest these things and Thou dost suffer them, and Thou dost not say to us what we are to do to them in regard to these.'

Then said the Most High, the Holy and Great One spake, and sent Uriel to the son of Lamech, and said to him:

'Go to Noah and tell him in my name "Hide thyself!" and reveal to him the end that is approaching, that the whole earth will be destroyed, and a deluge is about to come upon the whole earth, and will destroy all that is on it.

And now instruct him that he may escape and his seed may be preserved for all the generations of the world.'

And again the Lord said to Raphael:

'Bind Azazel hand and foot, and cast him into the darkness, and make an opening in the desert, which is in Dudael, and cast him therein.

And place upon him rough and jagged rocks, and cover him with darkness, and let him abide there forever, and cover his face that he may not see light.

And on the day of the great judgment he shall be cast into the fire. And heal the earth which the angels have corrupted, and proclaim the healing of the earth, that they may heal the plague, and that all the children of men may not perish through all the secret things that the Watchers have disclosed and have taught their sons.

And the whole earth has been corrupted through the works that were taught by Azazel, to him ascribe all sin.'

And to Gabriel said the Lord:

'Proceed against the bastards and the reprobates, and against the children of fornication, and destroy the children of fornication and the children of the Watchers from amongst men and cause them to go forth, send them one against the other that they may destroy each other in battle, for length of days shall they not have.

And no request that they (i.e. their fathers) make of thee shall be granted unto their fathers on their behalf; for they hope to live an eternal life, and that each one of them will live five hundred years.'

And the Lord said unto Michael:

'Go, bind Semjaza and his associates who have united themselves with women so as to have defiled themselves with them in all their uncleanness.

And when their sons have slain one another, and they have seen the destruction of their beloved ones, bind them fast for seventy generations in the valleys of the earth, till the day of their judgment and of their consummation, till the judgment that is forever and ever is consummated.

In those days they shall be led off to the abyss of fire, and to the torment and the prison in which they shall be confined forever. And whosoever shall be condemned and destroyed will from thenceforth be bound together with them to the end of all generations.

And destroy all the spirits of the reprobate and the children of the Watchers, because they have wronged mankind. Destroy all wrong from the face of the earth and let every evil work come to an end, and let the plant of righteousness and truth appear, and it shall prove a blessing; the works of righteousness and truth shall be planted in truth and joy for evermore.

And then shall all the righteous escape, and shall live till they beget thousands of children, and all the days of their youth and their old age shall they complete in peace.

And then shall the whole earth be tilled in righteousness, and shall all be planted with trees and be full of blessing.

And all desirable trees shall be planted on it, and they shall plant vines on it, and the vine which they plant thereon shall yield wine in abundance, and as for all the seed which is sown thereon each measure of it shall bear a thousand, and each measure of olives shall yield ten presses of oil.

And cleanse thou the earth from all oppression, and from all unrighteousness, and from all sin, and from all godlessness, and all the uncleanness that is wrought upon the earth, destroy from off the earth.

And all the children of men shall become righteous, and all nations shall offer adoration and shall praise Me, and all shall worship Me. And the earth shall be cleansed from all defilement, and from all sin, and from all punishment, and from all torment, and I will never again send them upon it from generation to generation and forever.

And in those days I will open the store chambers of blessing which are in the heaven, so as to send them down upon the earth over the work and labor of the children of men.

And truth and peace shall be associated together throughout all the days of the world and throughout all the generations of men.'

Part III

The Dream Vision of Enoch

Enoch's Intercession for Azazel and the Fallen Angels

Enoch's Announcement to them of their First and Final Doom

Before these things Enoch was hidden, and no one of the children of men knew where he was hidden, and where he abode, and what had become of him.

And his activities had to do with the Watchers, and his days were with the holy ones.

And I, Enoch was blessing the Lord of majesty and the King of the ages, and lo! the Watchers called me--Enoch the scribe--and said to me:

> *'Enoch, thou scribe of righteousness, go, declare to the Watchers of the heaven who have left the high heaven, the holy eternal place, and have defiled themselves with women, and have done as the children of earth do, and have taken unto themselves wives, "Ye have wrought great destruction on the*

earth,

And ye shall have no peace nor forgiveness of sin, and inasmuch as they delight themselves in their children,

The murder of their beloved ones shall they see, and over the destruction of their children shall they lament, and shall make supplication unto eternity, but mercy and peace shall ye not attain".'

And Enoch went and said:

'Azazel, thou shalt have no peace, a severe sentence has gone forth against thee to put thee in bonds.

And thou shalt not have toleration nor request granted to thee, because of the unrighteousness which thou hast taught, and because of all the works of godlessness and unrighteousness and sin which thou hast shown to men.'

Then I went and spoke to them all together, and they were all afraid, and fear and trembling seized them.

And they besought me to draw up a petition for them that they might find forgiveness, and to read their petition in the presence of the Lord of heaven.

For from thenceforward they could not speak with Him nor lift up their eyes to heaven for shame of their sins for which they had been condemned.

Then I wrote out their petition, and the prayer in regard to their spirits and their deeds individually and in regard to their requests that they should have forgiveness and length of days.

And I went off and sat down at the waters of Dan, in the land of Dan, to the south of the west of Hermon, I read their petition till I fell asleep.

And behold a dream came to me, and visions fell down upon me, and I saw visions of chastisement, and a voice came bidding me I to tell it to the sons of heaven, and reprimand them.

And when I awaked, I came unto them, and they were all sitting gathered together, weeping in Abel's jail, which is between Lebanon and Seneser, with their faces covered.

And I recounted before them all the visions which I had seen in sleep, and I began to speak the words of righteousness, and to reprimand the heavenly Watchers.

The book of the words of righteousness, and of the reprimand of the eternal Watchers in accordance with the command of the Holy Great One in that vision.

I saw in my sleep what I will now say with a tongue of flesh and with the breath of my mouth, which the Great One has given to men to converse therewith and understand with the heart.

As He has created and given to man the power of

understanding the word of wisdom, so hath He created me also and given me the power of reprimanding the Watchers, the children of heaven.

I wrote out your petition, and in my vision it appeared thus, that your petition will not be granted unto you throughout all the days of eternity, and that judgment has been finally passed upon you, yea, your petition will not be granted unto you.

And from henceforth you shall not ascend into heaven unto all eternity, and in bonds of the earth the decree has gone forth to bind you for all the days of the world.

And that previously you shall have seen the destruction of your beloved sons and ye shall have no pleasure in them, but they shall fall before you by the sword.

And your petition on their behalf shall not be granted, nor yet on your own, even though you weep and pray and speak all the words contained in the writing which I have written.

And the vision was shown to me thus, Behold, in the vision clouds invited me and a mist summoned me, and the course of the angels and the lightnings sped and hastened me, and the winds in the vision caused me to fly and lifted me upward, and bore me into heaven.

And I went in till I drew nigh to a wall which is built of crystals and surrounded by tongues of fire, and it began to affright me. And I went into the tongues of fire and drew nigh to a large house which was built of crystals, and the walls of the house were like a tessellated floor, made of crystals, and its groundwork was of crystal.

Its ceiling was like the path of the angels and the lightnings, and between them were fiery cherubim, and their heaven was clear as water.

A flaming fire surrounded the walls, and its portals blazed with fire.

And I entered into that house, and it was hot as fire and cold as ice, there were no delights of life therein, fear covered me, and trembling got hold upon me.

And as I quaked and trembled, I fell upon my face.

And I beheld a vision, And lo! there was a second house, greater than the former, and the entire portal stood open before me, and it was built of flames of fire.

And in every respect it so excelled in splendor and magnificence and extent that I cannot describe to you its splendor and its extent.

And its floor was of fire, and above it were lightnings and the path of the angels, and its ceiling also was flaming fire.

And I looked and saw therein a lofty throne, its appearance was as crystal, and the wheels thereof as the shining sun, and there was the vision of cherubim.

And from underneath the throne came streams of flaming fire so that I could not look thereon.

And the Great Glory sat thereon, and His raiment shone more brightly than the sun and was whiter than any snow.

None of the angels could enter and could behold His face by reason of the magnificence and glory and no flesh could behold Him.

The flaming fire was round about Him, and a great fire stood before Him, and none around could draw nigh Him, ten thousand *times* ten thousand stood before Him, yet He needed no counselor.

And the most holy ones who were nigh to Him did not leave by night nor depart from Him.

And until then I had been prostrate on my face, trembling, and the Lord called me with His own mouth, and said to me:

'Come hither, Enoch, and hear my word.'

And one of the holy ones came to me and waked me, and He made me rise up and approach the door, and I bowed my face downwards.

And He answered and said to me, and I heard His voice:

'Fear not, Enoch, thou righteous man and scribe of righteousness, approach hither and hear my voice.

And go, say to the Watchers of heaven, who have sent thee to intercede for them, "You should intercede for men, and not men for you.

Wherefore have ye left the high, holy, and eternal heaven, and lain with women, and defiled yourselves with the daughters of men and taken to yourselves wives, and done like the children of earth, and begotten giants as your sons?

And though ye were holy, spiritual, living the eternal life, you have defiled yourselves with the blood of women, and have begotten children with the blood of flesh, and, as the children of men, have lusted after flesh and blood as those also do who die and perish.

Therefore have I given them wives also that they might impregnate them, and beget children by them, that thus nothing might be wanting to them on earth.

But you were formerly spiritual, living the eternal life, and immortal for all generations of the world.

And therefore I have not appointed wives for you; for as for the spiritual ones of the heaven, in heaven is their dwelling.

And now, the giants, who are produced from the spirits and flesh, shall be called evil spirits upon the earth, and on the earth shall be their dwelling.

Evil spirits have proceeded from their bodies; because they are born from men, and from the holy Watchers is their beginning and primal origin; they shall be evil spirits on earth, and evil spirits shall they be called.

As for the spirits of heaven, in heaven shall be their dwelling, but as for the spirits of the earth which were born upon the earth, on the earth shall be their dwelling.

And the spirits of the giants afflict, oppress, destroy, attack, do battle, and work destruction on the earth, and cause trouble, they take no food, but nevertheless hunger and thirst, and cause offences. And these spirits shall rise up against the children of men and against the women, because they have proceeded from them.

From the days of the slaughter and destruction and death of the giants, from the souls of whose flesh the spirits, having gone forth, shall destroy without incurring judgment--thus shall they destroy until the day of the consummation, the great judgment in which the age shall be consummated, over the Watchers and the godless, yea, shall be wholly consummated."

And now as to the Watchers who have sent thee to intercede for them, who had been aforetime in heaven, say to them, "You have been in heaven, but all the mysteries had not yet been revealed to you, and you knew worthless ones, and these in the hardness of your hearts you have made known to the women, and through these mysteries women and men work much evil on earth."

Say to them therefore: "You have no peace".'

Part IV

Enoch's First Journey

And they took and brought me to a place in which those who were there were like flaming fire, and, when they wished, they appeared as men.

And they brought me to the place of darkness, and to a mountain the point of whose summit reached to heaven.

And I saw the places of the luminaries and the treasuries of the angels and of the thunder and in the uttermost depths, where were a fiery bow and arrows and their quiver, and a fiery sword and all the lightnings.

And they took me to the living waters, and to the fire of the west, which receives every setting of the sun.

And I came to a river of fire in which the fire flows like water and discharges itself into the great sea towards the west.

I saw the great rivers and came to the great river and to the great darkness, and went to the place where no flesh walks.

I saw the mountains of the darkness of winter and the place whence all the waters of the deep flow.

I saw the mouths of all the rivers of the earth and the

mouth of the deep.

I saw the treasuries of all the winds, I saw how He had furnished with them the whole creation and the firm foundations of the earth.

And I saw the corner-stone of the earth, I saw the four winds which bear the earth and the firmament of the heaven.

And I saw how the winds stretch out the vaults of heaven, and have their station between heaven and earth, these are the pillars of the heaven.

I saw the winds of heaven which turn and bring the circumference of the sun and all the angels to their setting.

I saw the winds on the earth carrying the clouds, I saw the paths of the angels. I saw at the end of the earth the firmament of the heaven above. And I proceeded and saw a place which burns day and night, where there are seven mountains of magnificent stones, three towards the east, and three towards the south.

And as for those towards the east, one was of colored stone, and one of pearl, and one of jacinth, and those towards the south of red stone.

But the middle one reached to heaven like the throne of God, of alabaster, and the summit of the throne was of sapphire.

And I saw a flaming fire. And beyond these mountains is a region the end of the great earth, there the heavens were completed.

And I saw a deep abyss, with columns of heavenly fire, and among them I saw columns of fire fall, which were beyond measure alike towards the height and towards the depth.

And beyond that abyss I saw a place which had no firmament of the heaven above, and no firmly founded earth beneath it, there was no water upon it, and no birds, but it was a waste and horrible place.

I saw there seven angels like great burning mountains, and to me, when I inquired regarding them, the angel said:

> *'This place is the end of heaven and earth, this has become a prison for the angels and the host of heaven.*
>
> *And the angels which roll over the fire are they which have transgressed the commandment of the Lord in the beginning of their rising, because they did not come forth at their appointed times.*
>
> *And He was wroth with them, and bound them till the time when their guilt should be consummated even for ten thousand years.'*

And Uriel said to me:

> *'Here shall stand the angels who have connected themselves*

with women, and their spirits assuming many different forms are defiling mankind and shall lead them astray into sacrificing to demons as gods, here shall they stand, till the day of the great judgment in which they shall be judged till they are made an end of.

And the women also of the angels who went astray shall become sirens.'

And I, Enoch, alone saw the vision, the ends of all things, and no man shall see as I have seen.

Part V

The Name and Functions of the Seven Archangels

And these are the names of the holy angels who watch.

Uriel, one of the holy angels, who is over the world and over Tartarus.

Raphael, one of the holy angels, who is over the spirits of men.

Raguel, one of the holy angels who takes vengeance on the world of the luminaries.

Michael, one of the holy angels, to wit, he that is set over the best part of mankind and over chaos.

Saraqael, one of the holy angels, who is set over the spirits, who sin in the spirit.

Gabriel, one of the holy angels, who is over Paradise and the serpents and the Cherubim.

Remiel, one of the holy angels, whom God set over those who rise.

Part VI

Preliminary and Final Place of Punishment of the Fallen Angels

And I proceeded to where things were chaotic.

And I saw there something horrible, I saw neither a heaven above nor a firmly founded earth, but a place chaotic and horrible.

And there I saw seven angels of the heaven bound together in it, like great mountains and burning with fire.

Then I said:

> 'For what sin are they bound, and on what account have they been cast in hither?'

Then said Uriel, one of the holy angels, who was with me, and was chief over them, and said:

> 'Enoch, why dost thou ask, and why art thou eager for the truth?

> These are of the number of the angels of heaven, which have transgressed the commandment of the Lord, and are bound here till ten thousand years, the time entailed by their sins are

consummated.'

And from thence I went to another place, which was still more horrible than the former, and I saw a horrible thing, a great fire there which burnt and blazed, and the place was cleft as far as the abyss, being full of great descending columns of fire, neither its extent or magnitude could I see, nor could I conjecture.

Then I said:

'How fearful is the place and how terrible to look upon!'

Then Uriel answered me, one of the holy angels who was with me, and said unto me:

'Enoch, why hast thou such fear and affright?'

And I answered:

'Because of this fearful place, and because of the spectacle of the pain.'

And he said unto me:

'This place is the prison of the angels, and here they will be imprisoned forever.'

Part VII

Sheol, or the Underworld

And thence I went to another place, and he showed me in the west another great and high mountain and of hard rock.

And there were four hollow places in it, deep and very smooth, three of them were dark and one bright; and there was a fountain of water in its midst.

And I said:

> '*How smooth are these hollow places, and deep and dark to view.*'

Then Raphael answered, one of the holy angels who was with me, and said unto me:

> '*These hollow places have been created for this very purpose, that the spirits of the souls of the dead should assemble therein, yea that all the souls of the children of men should assemble here. And these places have been made to receive them till the day of their judgment and till their appointed period till the period appointed, till the great judgment comes upon them.*'

I saw the spirit of a dead man making suit, and his voice went forth to heaven and made suit.

And I asked Raphael the angel who was with me, and I said unto him:

'This spirit which maketh suit, whose is it, whose voice goeth forth and maketh suit to heaven?'

And he answered me saying:

'This is the spirit which went forth from Abel, whom his brother Cain slew, and he makes his suit against him till his seed is destroyed from the face of the earth, and his seed is annihilated from amongst the seed of men.'

Then I asked regarding all the hollow places:

'Why is one separated from the other?'

And he answered me saying:

'These three have been made that the spirits of the dead might be separated. And this division has been made for the spirits of the righteous, in which there is the bright spring of water.

And this has been made for sinners when they die and are buried in the earth and judgment has not been executed upon them in their lifetime.

Here their spirits shall be set apart in this great pain, till the great day of judgment, scourgings, and torments of the accursed forever, so that there may be retribution for their spirits. There He shall bind them forever.

And this division has been made for the spirits of those who make their suit, who make disclosures concerning their destruction, when they were slain in the days of the sinners.

And this has been made for the spirits of men who shall not be righteous but sinners, who are godless, and of the lawless they shall be companions, but their spirits shall not be punished in the day of judgment nor shall they be raised from thence.'

Then I blessed the Lord of Glory and said:

'Blessed art Thou, Lord of righteousness, who rulest over the world.'

Part VIII

The Fire That Deals With the Luminaries of Heaven

From thence I went to another place to the west of the ends of the earth.

And I saw a burning fire which ran without resting, and paused not from its course day or night but ran regularly.

And I asked saying:

'What is this which rests not?'

Then Raguel, one of the holy angels who was with me, answered me and said unto me:

'This course of fire which thou hast seen is the fire in the west which persecutes all the luminaries of heaven.'

Part IX

The Seven Mountains in the Northwest and the Tree of Life

And from thence I went to another place of the earth, and he showed me a mountain range of fire which burnt day and night.

And I went beyond it and saw seven magnificent mountains all differing each from the other, and the stones thereof were magnificent and beautiful, magnificent as a whole, of glorious appearance and fair exterior, three towards the east, one founded on the other, and three towards the south, one upon the other, and deep rough ravines, no one of which joined with any other.

And the seventh mountain was in the midst of these, and it excelled them in height, resembling the seat of a throne, and fragrant trees encircled the throne.

And amongst them was a tree such as I had never yet smelt, neither was any amongst them nor were others like it, it had a fragrance beyond all fragrance, and its leaves and blooms and wood wither not forever, and its fruit is beautiful, and its fruit resembles the dates of a palm.

Then I said:

'How beautiful is this tree, and fragrant, and its leaves are fair, and its blooms very delightful in appearance.'

Then answered Michael, one of the holy and honored angels who was with me, and was their leader.

And he said unto me:

'Enoch, why dost thou ask me regarding the fragrance of the tree, and why dost thou wish to learn the truth?'

Then I answered him saying:

'I wish to know about everything, but especially about this tree.'

And he answered saying:

'This high mountain which thou hast seen, whose summit is like the throne of God, is His throne, where the Holy Great One, the Lord of Glory, the Eternal King, will sit, when He shall come down to visit the earth with goodness.

And as for this fragrant tree no mortal is permitted to touch it till the great judgment, when He shall take vengeance on all and bring everything to its consummation forever. It shall then be given to the righteous and holy.

Its fruit shall be for food to the elect, it shall be transplanted to the holy place, to the temple of the Lord, the Eternal King.

Then shall they rejoice with joy and be glad,

And into the holy place shall they enter;
And its fragrance shall be in their bones,
And they shall live a long life on earth,
Such as thy fathers lived,
And in their days shall no sorrow or plague
Or torment or calamity touch them.'

Then blessed I the God of Glory, the Eternal King, who hath prepared such things for the righteous, and hath created them and promised to give to them.

Part X

Jerusalem and the Mountains, Ravines and Streams

And I went from thence to the middle of the earth, and I saw a blessed place in which there were trees with branches abiding and blooming of a dismembered tree.

And there I saw a holy mountain, and underneath the mountain to the east there was a stream and it flowed towards the south.

And I saw towards the east another mountain higher than this, and between them a deep and narrow ravine, in it also ran a stream underneath the mountain.

And to the west thereof there was another mountain, lower than the former and of small elevation, and a ravine deep and dry between them, and another deep and dry ravine was at the extremities of the three mountains.

And all the ravines were deep and narrow, being formed of hard rock, and trees were not planted upon them.

And I marveled at the rocks, and I marveled at the ravine, yea, I marveled very much.

Part XI

The Purpose of the Accursed Valley

Then said I:

'*For what object is this blessed land, which is entirely filled with trees, and this accursed valley between?*

Then Uriel, one of the holy angels who was with me, answered and said:

'*This accursed valley is for those who are accursed forever, Here shall all the accursed be gathered together who utter with their lips against the Lord unseemly words and of His glory speak hard things.*

Here shall they be gathered together, and here shall be the place of their habitation.

In the last times, in the days of the true judgment in the presence of the righteous forever, here shall the godly bless the Lord of Glory, the Eternal Kin.

In the days of judgment over the former, they shall bless Him for the mercy in accordance with which He has assigned them their lot.'

Then I blessed the Lord of Glory and set forth His glory and lauded Him gloriously.

Part XII

Enoch's Further Journey to the East

And thence I went towards the east, into the midst of the mountain range of the desert, and I saw a wilderness and it was solitary, full of trees and plants.

And water gushed forth from above.

Rushing like a copious watercourse, which flowed towards the northwest, it caused clouds and dew to ascend on every side.

And thence I went to another place in the desert, and approached to the east of this mountain range.

And there I saw aromatic trees exhaling the fragrance of frankincense and myrrh, and the trees also were similar to the almond tree.

And beyond these, I went afar to the east, and I saw another place, a valley full of water.

And therein there was a tree, the color of fragrant trees such as the mastic.

And on the sides of those valleys I saw fragrant cinnamon.

And beyond these I proceeded to the east.

And I saw other mountains, and amongst them were groves of trees, and there flowed forth from them nectar, which is named sarara and galbanum.

And beyond these mountains I saw another mountain to the east of the ends of the earth, whereon were aloe trees, and all the trees were full of stacte, being like almond trees.

And when one burnt it, it smelt sweeter than any fragrant odor.

And after these fragrant odors, as I looked towards the north over the mountains I saw seven mountains full of choice nard and fragrant trees and cinnamon and pepper.

And thence I went over the summits of all these mountains, far towards the east of the earth, and passed above the Erythraean Sea and went far from it, and passed over the angel Zotiel.

And I came to the Garden of Righteousness, and from afar off trees more numerous than these trees and great—two trees there, very great, beautiful, and glorious, and magnificent, and the tree of knowledge, whose holy fruit they eat and know great wisdom.

That tree is in height like the fir, and its leaves are like those of the Carob tree, and its fruit is like the clusters of the vine, very beautiful, and the fragrance of the tree penetrates afar.

Then I said:

'*How beautiful is the tree, and how attractive is its look!*'

Then Raphael the holy angel, who was with me, answered me and said:

'*This is the tree of wisdom, of which thy father old in years and thy aged mother, who were before thee, have eaten, and they learnt wisdom and their eyes were opened, and they knew that they were naked and they were driven out of the garden.*'

And from thence I went to the ends of the earth and saw there great beasts, and each differed from the other; and I saw birds also differing in appearance and beauty and voice, the one differing from the other.

And to the east of those beasts I saw the ends of the earth whereon the heaven rests, and the portals of the heaven open.

And I saw how the angels of heaven came forth, and I counted the portals out of which they proceed, and wrote down all their outlets, of each individual angel by itself, according to their number and their names, their courses and their positions, and their times and their months, as Uriel the holy angel who was with me showed me.

He showed all things to me and wrote them down for me, also their names he wrote for me, and their laws and their companies.

Part XIII

Enoch's Journey to the North

And from thence I went towards the north to the ends of the earth, and there I saw a great and glorious device at the ends of the whole earth.

And here I saw three portals of heaven open in the heaven, through each of them proceed north winds, when they blow there is cold, hail, frost, snow, dew, and rain.

And out of one portal they blow for good, but when they blow through the other two portals, it is with violence and affliction on the earth, and they blow with violence.

And from thence I went towards the west to the ends of the earth, and saw there three portals of the heaven open such as I had seen in the east, the same number of portals, and the same number of outlets.

Part XIV

Enoch's Journey to the South

And from thence I went to the south to the ends of the earth, and saw there three open portals of the heaven, and thence there come dew, rain, and wind.

And from thence I went to the east to the ends of the heaven, and saw here the three eastern portals of heaven open and small portals above them.

Through each of these small portals pass the angels of heaven and run their course to the west on the path which is shown to them.

And as often as I saw I blessed always the Lord of Glory, and I continued to bless the Lord of Glory who has wrought great and glorious wonders, to show the greatness of His work to the angels and to spirits and to men, that they might praise His work and all His creation, that they might see the work of His might and praise the great work of His hands and bless Him forever.

www.ingramcontent.com/pod-product-compliance
Lightning Source LLC
LaVergne TN
LVHW091210080426
835509LV00006B/927